Other titles from Dr. Nathaniel Stampley, Sr.

Parables of The Kingdom

Understanding Spiritual Gifts and Calling to Ministry

Biblical Commentary on Wisdom Literature

Introduction to
Homiletics

Copyright © 2017 Nathaniel Stampley

Spiritscribe Publishing, LLC
P.O. Box 2241
Humble, Texas 77347
www.spiritscribepublishing.com
(832) 445-6229

Stampley Ministries, Inc.
1036 W. Atkinson Avenue
Milwaukee, Wisconsin 53206
Phone: (414) 949-7568
Website: stampleyministries.org
Email: stampleyministries@gmail.com

ISBN 978-0-692-82028-5

Introduction to

Homiletics
(7 Sermons included)
The Art of Sermonizing

Dr. Nathaniel J. Stampley Sr., D. Min.

Table of Contents

Acknowledgments

Throughout our journey in life, the Creator has strategically placed individuals to assist us in fulfilling our purposes. The path to completing this publication started many years ago in my hometown: Baton Rouge, Louisiana.

Dr. John Mbiti once said, "I am because we are, and since we are; therefore, I am." I am eternally grateful for my saintly parents, James and Luetilda Stampley, for demonstrating the truest examples of what is ethical, practical, and spiritual. In addition to my parents, I was blessed with another set of parents: Vernon and Beatrice Reynolds (my wife's parents). In both cases, our parents were always there for us, filling in the space for our children and grandchildren. Thank you!

Next, I want to thank Elder Richmond Izard for the relentless hours he shared by using his eyes examining the material along with providing the footnotes and glossary. His contribution represents what it truly means to have a mentor-mentee relationship.

I want to thank the Heritage International Ministries Church of God in Christ and Least of These International (both based in Milwaukee, Wisconsin) for listening to many of these sermons over the years. I could not have asked for a better audience.

We give special thanks to our lovely children (6), sons-in-law (2), daughters-in-law (2), grandchildren (13) and brothers and sisters (9 remaining) for the endless support they have given.

Lastly, the journey of compiling this book has brought my lovely wife and me to the beautiful country of Belize (June 6-16, 2016). In Belize, I celebrated my 65th birthday, June 12, 2016. Carolyn and I have been married since July 29, 1972, and the bonding is growing each day. She provided the critical eyes for editing. After all, she is a retired English Teacher. We are delighted to introduce the first of a series of sermons. In addition, we will be sharing a series of religious and theological publications.

Introduction

In the summer of 1976, I was blessed to attend the Charles Harrison Mason[1] Theological Seminary, a Church of God in Christ educational institution of higher learning and an affiliate of the prestigious Interdenominational Theological Center of Atlanta, Georgia.

This experience helped reshape my theological views and also enabled me to become both a more articulate and disciplined minister[2]. Dr. Isaac Clark, an African Methodist Episcopal Minister and Professor of Homiletics, was a legendary figure and part of the heartbeat of that campus. He challenged every student to become more efficient in communication. I am eternally indebted to my mentor, Dr. Clark. This presentation is at the core of what Dr. Clark taught to thousands of students, including myself 40 years ago.

In my humble opinion, being summoned to proclaim the gospel is the ultimate profession in the world, and there is little or no tolerance for poorly prepared[3] ministers. Therefore, this course is designed to assist you in becoming an effective Ambassador for the Kingdom of God by mastering the art of communication[4]. Also, this publication will assist laity and

---

[1] Bishop Charles Harrison Mason is the founder of the Church of God in Christ.

[2] A *minister* is a servant, diplomatic representative, an agent, or ambassador.

[3] For every minute of time spent preaching, you should have spent at least one hour of preparatory work in prayer, meditation, research, and study. "Study to shew thyself approved unto God, a workman that needeth not to be ashamed, rightly dividing the word of truth." (2 Tim 2:15)

[4] Communication is the act of sending and receiving a message or an idea; the imparting or interchange of thoughts, opinions, or information by speech, writing, or signs. The process involves a sender (preacher), message (sermon), channel (spoken, written, nonverbal, etc.), and receiver (audience). Distribution channels include such avenues as live delivery, written sermons, sermonic

those outside the faith community to understand and appreciate the written word.

What is Homiletics?

Homiletics is the art[5] or discipline of preparing and delivering a sermon. Preaching or sermonizing is the process of liberating the hearer by means of "proclaiming" or presenting a conversation or animated story based upon biblical truths through the power and anointing of the Holy Spirit. The presenter extracts from a single source (usually the Bible) and displays one's rhetorical[6] skills (writing and speech) and constructs a theological discourse. Therefore, the listeners will receive both information and inspiration.[7] Effective preaching must be grounded in creativity. "Knowledge is like a garden, but if it is not cultivated, it cannot be harvested." (African Proverb)

---

transcripts, hardcopy and electronic books, audio and video recordings as well as live and constantly broadcast Internet streaming, podcasting, radio, and television. All forms of communication are important for an effective minister—oral and written as well as nonverbal. Messages that God speaks through you may be memorialized via written documents (as were epistles) and presently through audio and video recordings as well. The living word is not restricted by time or locality.

[5] Art deals with aesthetics (beauty) and creative expression. The word "aesthetic" comes from the Greek word *aisthētikos*, which means "perceptible by the senses," derived from *aisthesthai* to perceive.

[6] *Rhetoric* is the study of the effective use of language; the art of making persuasive speeches; oratory.

[7] The chief difference in teaching verses preaching is that preaching must "liberate." In other words, preaching sets the captive free. Expressed another way, preaching does everything that teaching does and additionally liberates through exhortation. Hence, the preacher must connect to the mind, soul, and spirit of the hearer by the power of the Holy Spirit.

Contents of a Sermon

I.   *Text/Scripture*

The selection of the text is very important. The text should be read in the context of a paragraph[8] in order to capture the essence of what is being conveyed. Please, remember the term *homiletics,*[9] which stems from the word *homo* and denotes a single or same source. It is acceptable to utilize a series of scriptures from multiple chapters during a bible class or other settings. However, based upon the techniques of Dr. Clark, it is best to build the sermon from a single source.

Prayer

A prayer is recommended after you read the text.

II.   *Subject*

Your subject (title) is not your text, and your text is not your subject. The subject is very important. An inappropriate subject can immediately cause you to lose your audience. A subject should always be positive. For example, *Keys to Overcoming a Sinful Life* is fine. However, it is inappropriate to use *Living in Sin* as a subject. A subject should never be a complete sentence but, rather, a *catch phrase,* which appears to be very effective. The title of the sermon should not exceed seven (7) words. Selecting a subject should come after you have prayed, pondered, and diagnosed the problem (which is located in your introduction).

---

[8] Not a literary or literal paragraph, but a section of text (number of verses) comprising a sub-story, topic, or complete thought. For example, many translations, such as the NKJV, NIV, and ESV insert descriptive headings boldly within the text to define paragraphic divisions.

[9] Homily: a Catholic term for a sermon, usually on a Biblical topic and usually of a non-doctrinal nature.

III. Introduction

An effective minister will consult more than the Bible[10] and should always have other references[11] on hand. A few suggestions include a thesaurus, an expository dictionary of biblical words,[12] and perhaps ancient and contemporary literature may be useful.

A. Story

I usually begin this section with a brief story in a manner similar to Jesus using parables. The minister must be creative which requires a little critical research in order to open the heart and pique the interest of the listeners.

B. Context

For example, you are encouraged to give general remarks about the book you selected (larger context). In addition, share remarks with the congregation about the content of the subject matter including the preceding and immediate chapters you have chosen.

---

[10] A study bible can serve as a precursory or introductory starting point for "Biblical exegesis" (drawing out the meaning from the written *text*) and "hermeneutics" (the wider defined discipline and study of interpretation theory involving all forms of communication, as well as everything in the interpretative process including verbal and nonverbal forms of communication as well as prior aspects that affect communication, such as presuppositions, pre-understandings, the meaning and philosophy of language, and semiotics).

Nowadays, countless translations of the bible, as well as numerous other companion resources, are available online at sites such as www.biblegateway.com, live.e-sword.net, www.crosswalk.com, and net.bible.org, just to name a few. These sites have sermon aids, commentaries, and other valuable tools.

[11] www.wikipedia.com, www.dictionary.com, www.thesaurus.com, and www.brainyquote.com are useful online resources (encyclopedia, dictionary, and thesaurus) for researching terminology, persons, and concepts.

[12] For example, *Vine's Complete Expository Dictionary of Old and New Testament Words*

C. Problem Statement

Your introduction is also the section where the problem is laid out (similar to a thesis statement). You should lay out the negative reason that inspired you to deliver this statement in the "what, how, why" format (Dr. Clark). Your problem statement is essential.

For example: *"It appears to me an alarming number of born-again believers have allowed Satan to creep deceptively from their past into their present (what), by means of polluting and defiling the sanctity of their bodies, which is the holy temple of God, with all kinds of wicked thoughts and abominable actions (how), all because perverse and ungodly desires are creeping into their minds and souls through open wounds in their flesh that are caused by latent* [13] *experiences that become backdoors to all kinds of sin (why)."* [14]

IV. Proposition

Generally speaking, a proposition is a plan or scheme[15] suggested for acceptance. I can hear Dr. Clark saying, "If it ain't got a proposition, then you ain't got a sermon." This is the pivotal juncture in your sermon because herein lies a brief (but convincing) opportunity to amplify a reason as to why the listeners should take heed to what you are saying.[16]

---

[13] Latent: dormant, hidden, and concealed.

[14] The illustrated problem statement is derived from the vision revealed by God to Ezekiel 8:7-9: of his prophetic writing: **"And [the Lord] brought me to the door of the court; and when I looked, behold a hole in the wall. Then said he unto me, Son of man, dig now in the wall: and when I had digged in the wall, behold a door..."**

[15] A *scheme* is a systematic plan for a course of action, a secret plot, a diagram, or outline.

[16] In other words, a proposition is the bridging of sound logic through deductive reasoning, which flows from a properly advanced major premise that compels an individual to accept a logical conclusion based upon the minor premises that will follow in the body points.

For example, to merely say, *"a person will go to hell if they do not take heed"* will not necessarily get someone's attention. However, if you creatively demonstrate how they are being taken advantage of in a situation, it usually gets their attention. This is also the place where you can introduce numerical references as a means of methodically putting forth corrective measures or points regarding the errors at hand.

V. Body

This component is extremely important because you are expected to present anywhere from two to four directives: points, things, suggestions, or perspectives. It is imperative that the presenter delivers this section in a positive manner.

VI. Conclusion

Lastly, wrap up your sermon by reiterating the aforementioned components such as the text, subject, introduction, proposition, and body. Be brief but thorough. It is also appropriate to climax your message with a story.

Two Types of Sermons

1. Text Led

The first type of sermon occurs as a result of browsing or studying the scriptures when there is a sudden sense of urgency to construct a sermon. Because of this inspiration, you must explore the circumstances surrounding the text (who, what, when, where, how, and why). For instance, a skilled minister or laity will incorporate exegesis, hermeneutics, historical, social, economic, political, and spiritual realities in the research (See footnote 10 on page 5).

Deductive reasoning is reasoning from the general to the particular (or from cause to effect).

2.   Life Led

The second type of sermon comes about as a result of coming face-to-face with an experience that inspires you to develop a sermon. For example, a trip to the devastated area of Hurricane Katrina or a face-to-face encounter with a homeless person may inspire you to construct a sermon.

Three Major Emphases for Delivering a Sermon

1.   Doing Sermon

This message is primarily aimed at *motivating* the listeners to put forth a diligent effort towards embracing and fulfilling a specific task at hand: new church, vans, choir robes etc. For example, an appropriate text might be "I can do all things through Christ who strengthens me" (Philippians 4:13).

2.   Thinking Sermon

This sermon is delivered to persuade the listener to *consider* or *ponder* over a particular area of growth pertaining to displaying godly character. For example, an appropriate text might be, "…If there be any virtue, and if there be any praise, think on these things" (Philippians 4:8).

3.   Being Sermon

This type of sermon is delivered more often than any of the others. Its purpose and mandate is to convince the hearer to make an *ultimate decision*. Therefore, a systematic[17] and persuasive approach is launched. For example, the minister may urge the congregation to *recognize, accept, and rely* on God. Such types of sermons are redemptive in nature. For example, "For what will profit it a man, if he gains the whole world, and forfeits his own soul?" (Matthew 16:26)

---

[17] Systematic: characterized by order and planning; methodical; careful; skillful; detailed; meticulous.

12

What Makes a Good Sermon?[18]

Duane Kelderman, Professor of Preaching at Calvin Theological Seminary, surveyed his adult education students for a few years. He asked the question, "What makes a good sermon?" Professor Kelderman summarized the answers, which fall into three clusters of responses relating to 1) communicational excellence, 2) biblical faithfulness, and 3) transformational power:

Communicational Excellence: "A good sermon is one that I can follow. The main point of the sermon is clear [and] well organized...The preacher does not speak over my head [or] repeat the same point over and over. The preacher uses...stories to keep me listening."

Biblical Faithfulness: "A good sermon is rooted in the Scripture...A good sermon is not the opinion of the preacher; it is a Word from God that has authority because it's from the Word of God."

Transformational Power! "A good sermon changes me...challenges me...stretches me. . . draws me closer to God... [and] deepens my faith." The challenge of the preacher is to apply not just one or two but all three criteria as we are following the anointed voice of the Holy Spirit.

Conclusion

The art of communication is clearly designed to express thought from one person to another. The minister or laity must be thorough, persuasive, and efficient at all times when delivering a sermon. My spiritual roots are embedded in the Pentecostal holiness experience, and I know firsthand that it is challenging to abandon old habits and embrace new techniques. The sermon[19] is a minister's artistic expression; wherein, the

---

[18] Duane Kelderman, "What Make's A Good Sermon?" *Calvin Theological Seminary Forum* (Spring 2002): 9

[19] Although it is the artistic expression of the minister, every effective sermon must be both spirit-led and true to the text.

minister skillfully and convincingly persuades individuals to consider entering the Kingdom[20] of God. The minister must be well equipped and never display ignorance due to a lack of preparation. There is no greater honor than fulfilling a call to the ministry. "When the student is ready, the teacher will appear."

Glossary of Key Terms

ART: dealing with creative self-expression. *(See "What is Homiletics?" pg. 7)*

AESTHETICS: concerning art, pertaining to the study of beauty, emotions and sensation. *(See "What is Homiletics?" pg. 7)*

COMMUNICATION: The act of sending and receiving a message or idea; the imparting or interchange of thoughts, opinions, or information by speech, writing, or signs. *(See "Introduction," pg.1)*

DEDUCTION: Deductive reasoning is a process of reasoning or logic in which a conclusion follows necessarily from the premises presented, so that the conclusion cannot be false if the premises are true. *(See "IV. Proposition," pg. 10)*

---

[20] A *kingdom* (Hebrew *malkut & mamlakah*; Greek *basileia*) is a form of governmental rule that deals with 1.) territory (vast, spatial) and 2.) authority (sovereignty, dominion, royalty, power, majesty, throne, judgment, law, reign). In *God's Big Idea*, authored by Dr. Myles Munroe, a kingdom is defined as "a kingdom is the governing influence of a king over a territory, impacting it with his will, his purpose and his intent, to produce a citizenry of people who reflect the king's morals, values, language, and culture."

EXEGESIS: To *"exegete"* is to "draw out" the meaning from the written text. *(See "III. Introduction" on pg. 9 and "1. Tex t Led," pg. 11)*

HERMENEUTICS: The science (discipline and study) of interpretation. *(See "III. Introduction" on pg. 9 and "1.Text Led," pg. 11)*

HOMILETICS: The art or discipline of preparing and delivering a sermon, "preaching" or "sermonizing." *(See "What is Homiletics?" pg. 6 and "Preaching," below)*

HOMILY: Catholic terminology for a *sermon*, usually on a Biblical topic and usually of a non-doctrinal nature.

INDUCTION: *Inductive reasoning* is a process of reasoning, used especially in science, by which a general conclusion is drawn from a set of premises, based mainly on experience or experimental evidence. The conclusion goes beyond the information contained in the premises and does not follow necessarily from them. Thus, an inductive argument may be highly probable, yet lead from true premises to a false conclusion. *(Compare with "Deduction," above)*

KINGDOM: "A kingdom is the governing influence of a king over a territory, impacting it with his will, his purpose, and his intent to produce a citizenry of people who reflect the king's morals, values, language, and culture." *(See pg. 8)*

Conclusion: *(See pg. 8)*

KINGDOM OF GOD: The unrestricted and boundless spiritual place where The Most High God dwells and governs with authority and unparalleled power. The Kingdom of God may consist of people, places, and things, but in actuality it must be clearly understood that this Kingdom transcends the carnal and physical spheres of life. Apostle Paul elaborates on the essence of the Kingdom in Romans 14: 17. *(See "Kingdom," above and the publication, "Kingdom of God: Twelve Lessons" by Dr. Stampley)*

MINISTER: A servant, diplomatic representative, an agent, or ambassador. *(See "Introduction," pg. 6)*

PREACHING: Preaching or sermonizing is the process of liberating the hearer by means of "proclaiming" or presenting a conversation or animated story based upon Biblical Truths through the power and anointing of the Holy Spirit. *(See "What is Homiletics?" pg. 7)*

PROPOSITION: A proposed plan or scheme of a logical argument that suggests something for consideration, acceptance, adoption, or completion. *(See "IV.Proposition," pg. 4)*

RHETORIC: The study of the effective use of language; the art of making persuasive speeches; oration. *(See "What is Homiletics?" pg. 7)*

SCHEME: A systematic plan for a course of action, a secret plot, a diagram, or outline. *(See "IV. Proposition," pg. 4)*

SERMON:	A minister's artistic expression wherein the minister skillfully and convincingly persuades individuals to enter the Kingdom of God via the power of the Holy Spirit. *(See ".*
SYSTEMATIC:	Characterized by the use of order and planning; methodical; careful; skillful; detailed; meticulous. *(See "IV.Proposition," pg. 10)*

Now, in order for you to understand and appreciate this creative and effective format of homiletics, I will introduce seven (7) sermons based upon the six major components. Three of these sermons will be presented in an outline format whereby this will enable you to get acquainted with the technique. The outlined sermons are entitled: *Never Saw Anything like This; The Three Pillars of the Church; What Really Happened on that Day.* Next, I have prepared a four-part sermon entitled **Demonstrations of Faith and Deliverance.**

The discipline of scholarship and research must be restored in the faith community. This book kicks off a series of sermons that hopefully will inspire and inform you regarding the people, geography, situations and spiritual mandates associated with these Biblical Stories.

Sermon Outlines

Subject: **Never Saw Anything like This**

Text: Mark 2:1-12 3/17/10; 6/25/11; 8/24/14; 8/2/15

III. Introduction

Story: There was a hound dog laying in the yard. An old man in overalls was sitting on the porch. "Excuse me sir, but does your dog bite?" the tourist asked. The old man replied, "Nope."

So, the tourist stepped out of his car. The dog ran over snarling, growling, and bit him on his arms and legs. As the dog was dragging him away, the tourist was flailing around in the dust and yelled, "I thought you said your dog didn't bite!"

The old man replied, "Ain't my dog."

I suggest you pay attention to what you are asking, what is being said, and (by all means) do not make assumptions.

Larger Context:

➢ Mark, Matthew, and Luke are commonly called the Synoptic Gospel.

➢ Traditionally, it is held Peter (an eyewitness and disciple of Jesus) dictated the Lamb's teaching to John and Mark. Initially, this gospel account was recorded somewhere around 50 A.D. (most likely in Rome).

➢ The central theme of the book presents and defends Jesus' universal call to discipleship.

➢ Jesus is the Son of God and the Son of Man, and he brings clarity to the role of the Messiah.

➢ There is sense of urgency and secrecy occurring throughout Jesus' ministry.

➢ Jesus not only addressed the spiritual needs in

➢ Galilee, but he also addressed the physical needs therefore creating a wholesome deliverance.

➢ Roman occupation and inadequate religious representation helped create an oppressed situation for the masses.

➢ "When the condition for growth is met, then growth follows, automatically." (Thurman)

➢ Jesus seized the opportunity to teach profound lessons regarding the Kingdom of God throughout Galilee.

Smaller Context: Chapter 2 introduces Jesus in his adopted home, Capernaum, retreating after spending time away from preaching, teaching, and healing. Let us assume he returned to his residence to relax or regroup for a brief period.

The Problem

It appears to me a disturbing number of people both within and without the faith, community, are finding themselves facing challenging situations, by means of being unable to personally correct the problem while not seeing a cooperative effort to assist in bringing about a change, due to Satan, who has created a false sense of security, selfishness, or spiritual immaturity when it comes to going to Jesus for help.

Comments on the scriptures:

Verse 1: The word spreads rapidly that Jesus has returned home.

Verse 2: Shortly thereafter, both the interior and exterior of the home was filled to capacity. Jesus understands his mission to proclaim the Gospel of the Kingdom. His notoriety and spiritual authority were already established.

Verse 3: There were many needs: spiritual, mental, and physical, but for some reason a paralytic appeared on the scene accompanied by four men. I love the idea that they pondered what was best for the sick man and decided to take him to Jesus.

Verse 4: They were unable to gain access to see Jesus due to the crowd; therefore, the group decided to create an entrance through the roof. Generally speaking, the homes had flat roofs consisting of branches and sticks combined with clay tiles. At any rate, the roof had to be damaged without permission due to the urgency of the matter in order to carry out this plan. Sometimes, you have to do unusual things in order to get favorable results.

Verse 5: This spectacular entry is depicted as an act of faith and definitely got the attention of Jesus in the midst of ministering. Jesus was so impressed with this gesture; it is worth noting how he replied, "Son, your sins are forgiven." Several things are revealed in this statement. Jesus identifies or relates to the man by calling him "son." Jesus' humanity and divinity stands out. Jesus addressed the spiritual needs over the physical conditions. Jesus' direct statement regarding forgiveness indicates who He really is, just like what the man really needed.

Verse 6: Whenever, we observe the manifestation of God (glory), you can rest assure critics, skeptics, and self-righteous individuals will be waiting nearby to respond. Meanwhile, the scribes, teachers, or religious authorities on the Torah/Law perceived what Jesus said without saying anything, but Christ noted their demeanor.

Verse 7: Their ill thoughts toward Jesus were very strong. You know how you can be in a room where people do not want your presence although they are not saying a word? Obviously, they could not discern Jesus is the Messiah and manifestation of God because He appears to be a mere, mortal man.

Verse 8: Jesus could not take it any longer, and he immediately nips this in the bud by letting them know He is aware of their thoughts. He goes on to try and teach them about eternal matters. In other words, Jesus fulfills the role of a prophet: discerning and instructing.

Verse 9: Jesus puts forth a couple of questions in order to help these so-called, learned men understand what is really going on. Which statement is the most appropriate? "Your sins are forgiven?" or "rise, take up your bed and walk?" These statements contain the temporal and eternal converging at the same time or the visible and invisible converging on this man. Forgiveness reconciles us with God while physical restoration alone will not cause you to be at peace with God. Jesus gave the man both because his faith moved Christ to deem him worthy.

Verse 10: Jesus continues his teaching before the crowd, scribes, man, friends, and the disciples by disclosing He is the *Son of Man*. In this role, he has come to serve or minister to those whom the religious leaders and society as a whole has abandoned. In addition, he has come to extend forgiveness and usher in reconciliation.

Verse 11: After clarifying or making sense out of the nonsense caused by the Scribes, Jesus continues with the issue at hand by telling the disabled man, "Rise, pick up your bed, and go home." After all, the man was created to walk instead of being carried around by others. This freedom (physically and spiritually) served as a commission to leave this place and spread the good news to others at home and elsewhere.

Verse 12: The man was brought in through abnormal means (roof) by friends with compassion, but he is leaving through a normal channel (door) where everyone is able to see and witness. The man was thankful and amazed, and the people glorified or exalted God for the miracle unfolding before their very eyes.

Earlier, Jesus was amazed to see the unusual faith of lowering a man through the roof, and now the people are amazed to see what Jesus has done for this man. They said, "We never saw anything like this!" This reactionary phrase clearly serves as an attention grabber or eye opener to something extraordinary. The statement can be viewed positively or negatively just like the glass of water appears to be half full or half empty.

Contemporary Analysis

> ➢ On March 3, 2010, I returned from my 2nd mission trip to Haiti along with seven members of our mission team.
> ➢ Life in Haiti was interrupted due to a major earthquake thus leaving hundreds of thousands dead and a country in disarray.

- We saw a poor and inadequate infrastructure trying to handle the massive outpouring of support from around the world.
- We saw overcrowded marketplaces and people in the street crying out for help while utilizing what they already had to work with.
- Contrary to the painful images we saw in the media, we also saw breathtaking scenes of beautiful mountains, vegetation, and beaches.
- We also observed dead bodies that had not been discovered and people lined up for medical and food supplies.
- We saw a nation laying in ruin coupled with a rainy season causing more damage and problems.
- Since 1989, I have supported one disaster after another i.e. Louisiana, Mississippi, Alabama, Georgia, Oklahoma, Missouri, etc. resulting in thousands of displaced families.
- I see public schools being inadequately funded and being neglected all across the USA, especially in urban areas.
- I see violence and crime running rampant in the inner cities of America, and we are becoming too comfortable with these unnecessary deaths. Putting it another way, far too many of our youth do not expect to live pass forty.
- I see little, innocent children in foster care and adoption agencies waiting to be loved and given an opportunity.
- I see a political system headed by democrats and republicans who have basically disconnected from the needs of the people. I see politics before principles.
- I see churches in abundance and diverse religious practices, but I am looking for the character of Jesus to show up in these ministries in many cases.
- I see more and more young African and Latino Americans being marched off to prison instead of investing in the social and economic developments in their communities.
- The poor not only deserve food, clothing, shelter, and medical care, but they also appreciate aesthetics and the opportunity to be creative.

- I can go on and on with these dismal realities, but I also want to see family and friends taking these realities to Jesus like we see in this story.
- "The ultimate measure of a man is not where he stands in moments of comforts and convenience but where he stands at times of challenge and controversy." (MLK Jr.)

I see truth and freedom waiting to be discovered by those with a passion for change and deliverance. I see a ministry, Heritage, where members and others are asked to step up to the plate and do a little more, but it begins with a life of faith. Faith requires awareness, effort, and compassion because you will see good results in the end.

IV. Proposition

Have you ever been on your way to a significant event or found yourself doing something very important but confronted with an unusual interruption? The way you handle this situation can build faith and character. Interruptions and challenges are inevitable, so you might as well be prepared to face them. Therefore, our text suggests three perspectives that should be considered since I believe all of you prefer a favorable ending. Hereafter, you will truly understand what is meant by *Never Saw Anything like This*.

V. Body

1. Wake up and recognize how God seems to always present opportunities in order for the liberating gospel of the kingdom to go forth by means of making yourself willing to alter your personal plans and utilize the comforts of home and elsewhere as springboards for teaching and preaching, so that you may establish a foundation for deliverance, hope, and understanding while saying *Never Saw Anything like This or Simply Amazing*.

2. God masterfully presents these opportunities for each of you to assist others by going the extra mile in terms of eliminating excuses and pressing through the challenges until you arrive at the place of help. This occurs simply because it will allow your faith to   grow

24

alongside others who are also witnesses to the manifestation of God and say *Never Saw Anything like This or Simply Amazing.*

3. Finally, for every significant moment in your life, you must brace yourself for the critics and naysayers. This means what they say and do must be viewed as stepping stones and building blocks in your walk of faith all because the virtues of faith and love cannot be destroyed but rather they will propel you into the arena of spiritual fulfillment and enable you to say *Never Saw Anything like This or Simply Amazing.*

VI. Conclusion

I delight in challenging others to stay focused and humble. I have tried to show you things will occur i.e. sickness, disease, and calamities, but God seems to provide avenues or vehicles of escape for every adversity.

Let me close with a story entitled "Three Bullets." There was once a man who had nothing for his family to eat. He had an old rifle and three bullets. So, he decided to go hunting and kill some wild game for dinner.

As he went down the road, he saw a rabbit. He shot at the rabbit and missed it. The rabbit ran away. Then he saw a squirrel and fired a shot at the squirrel but missed it. The squirrel disappeared into a hole in a cottonwood tree.

As he went further, he saw a large wild 'Tom' turkey in the tree, but he had only one bullet remaining. A voice spoke to him and said, *"Pray first, aim high, and stay focused.*

However, he saw a deer which was a better kill at that time. He brought the gun down and aimed at the deer. But, then he saw a rattlesnake between his legs about to bite him, so he naturally brought the gun down further to shoot the rattlesnake.

Still, the voice repeated to him, "I said, *pray, aim high, and stay focused.* So, the man decided to listen to God's voice. He prayed, then aimed the gun high up in the tree, and   shot the wild turkey. The bullet bounced off the turkey and killed the deer. The handle fell off the gun, hit the snake in the head, and killed it. And when the gun had gone off, it knocked him into a pond.

When he stood up to look around, he had fish in all of his pockets, a dead deer, and a turkey for his family to eat. The snake (Satan) was dead simply because the man listened to God.

Essence of the story: Pray before you do anything. Aim and shoot high in your goals and stay focused on God. Never let others discourage you based upon what happened in your past. "It is not the size of the dog in the fight but the size of the fight in the dog." The past is exactly that: the past. Live and learn one day at a time. Plus, remember only God knows the future, and He will not put you through any more than you can bear. Do not look to man for your blessings, but look to the doors that only He has prepared in advance for you in your favor, and God will provide all of the assistance when the heart and conditions are truly lined up like we see in the text and this story. If you must do something bizarre or different, by all means, let it be for a good cause.

The Three Pillars:
Love, Holiness, and Hope

Jude 1: 17-23 12/26/10 & 5/5/13

I. **Story** - One day, a small elephant was captured and tied to the end of a long chain around its foot. The other end was tied to a very large, rubber tree. Initially, the young elephant would pull with all its strength, but it was unable to get free. Finally, after several weeks of struggling, he surrenders to the chain and conditions. At this point, the hunter takes the elephants and chains it to a little iron stake by a circus tent. By this time, the elephant never attempts to pull away because it thinks it's chained to a rubber tree. You see the elephant never realizes how easy it is to break away. It has given up and surrendered to its circumstances. Each of you must learn from this story by not allowing circumstances to cause you to give up.

II. **Introduction** -This book is the shortest book in the New Testament regarding Church Doctrines, yet it is seldom read. The book is presumed to be written by the brothers of James and Jesus. The primary theme and occasion permeates around the saints watching out for false teaching and contend for the faith. Apparently, the congregation was mixed with Jews and Gentiles thus serving as a prime target for Gnostics and heretical sects and groups to infiltrate. Jude draws analogies by referring to Old Testament situations that resulted in divine judgment. In the verses prior to our text, it is interesting to note Jude makes reference to Enoch, a book found in the Apocrypha. We estimate the book was written in the mid 60's

A.D.

III. **Problem** - *It appears to me there is far   too much   apathy   and   tolerance   for unrighteous and unethical behavior within the community of faith, by means of displaying profane hatred and doubt while yet claiming to be a follower of Christ, due to Satan masterfully deceiving and luring you from the three pillars: holiness, love, and faith.*

IV. **Overview of our text**

> Verses 17-23 can be labeled A Call to Persevere.

> Verses 17-19 give us an Apostolic warning to the church.

> The writer addressed the congregants as *Beloved, which* indicates a group of believers having a special relationship with Christ.

> The Greek term *Agapetos* refers to a chosen group whom Christ loves, and they express that love to one another.

> The church is admonished to remember the teachings of the Apostles regarding the last days (Eschaton).

> The last days refer to the extreme or utmost period from the initial proclamation of the Gospel of the Kingdom spoken by Jesus Christ. The end times also reflect a heightened period of promiscuous, sensuous, and unethical behavior.

to *Scoffers/Mockers*. The Greek term *Ekmukterizo* denotes holding one's nose up in derision at someone; to mock or make fun of. In other words, this period will be marked by the justification, tolerance, and glamorization of sin and evil i.e. adultery, fornication, and homosexuality.

> These ungodly passions clearly display a disregard or reverence for God and His righteousness.

> Whenever we see ungodly acts amongst us, then rest assured, there is a spirit behind it that is grounded in division. Ungodly and worldly people have the ability to negatively influence the godly thus causing them to depart from the faith.

> Verse 20: Jude reminds them of who they are and what is expected of them. The beloved of Christ are expected to build upon the pillars and foundation of the kingdom i.e. holiness, love, and faith.

> It is imperative to take note of the blueprint for construction and the materials you use to build. Jude makes it crystal clear that Christ is the eternal foundation.

> If there is holy faith, then there can be profane and secular faith. The church is expected to be separate and devoted to Christ by displaying unwavering faith. There cannot be a mixture of faith in Christ and Gnosticism or any other strange doctrines.

> Afterward, we are admonished to place praying alongside our faith. This spiritual exercise is grounded in honoring, petitioning, and asking God to rule on our behalf in a manner that brings glory to Him.

> In order to pray effectively, we must welcome and allow the Holy Spirit (Pneuma

& Hagios) to govern and guide us in all we ask or think.

➢ Verse 21 is so important because we need to understand what is meant by "Keep yourself in the love of God." In other words, we are to guard our character at all times through prayer, embracing sound doctrines, and patiently waiting for the Lord's return.

Once you properly align yourself (spiritually speaking), then, you can expect favorable results from the Lord. In the judicial courts, the defendant who presents all of the evidence and demonstrates humility may be guilty in the end and expect some leniency from the judge. Likewise, if you construct your life around faith, praying, love, and patience, then it makes sense to look for the mercies of God to come your way. The New Testament term *Eleos* refers to the outward manifestation of pity because it assumes need on the part of him who receives it and adequate resources for meeting needs of him who shows it.

The righteous must remain humble and resilient in order to ultimately experience eternal life. This reminds me of a story about a young teenager who decided to quit school because he was bored with classes. His father tried desperately to convince him to stay in school. "Son," he said, "You can't quit. History is loaded with examples of great leaders who are remembered because they did not quit. Martin L. King, Jr. did not quit. Booker T. Washington, George W. Carver, and Carter G. Woodson did not quit, and Willie Johnson did not quit."

"Who?" the son burst in. "Who in the world is Willie Johnson?"

"See," the father replied, "You don't remember him because he quit." The lesson from life is that we only remember those who persist.

Not only are you expected to mature spiritually and safeguard yourselves from ungodly activities, but you are also expected to help others who find themselves entrapped.

Doubt is a reality; therefore, we are asked to have mercy and display patience with those who display this behavior. Thank God for where you may be, but how about helping others who are not at that level? Doubt is usually due to a lack of knowledge, negative experiences, or the inability to move forward. Usually, a little encouragement and love goes a long way with a doubter.

The writer goes on to ask us to remember and assist others beyond the doubters. Have you ever had to literally go and get someone out of trouble or harm's way i.e. drug house, prostitution, abusive relationship, and hanging with the wrong crowd? Sin leaves a stain (garment of stain); therefore, we must utilize every means necessary

31

to show men and women a more excellent way. You can talk and reason with some people, while you literally have to snatch others from where they are in order to create an atmosphere for deliverance.

V. Contemporary Realities and Parallels

➤ The church community has been infiltrated with too many negative images from the pulpit to the door.

➤ I wonder how many people truly know and understand the Doctrines of the Church.

➤ Do you know the difference between principles and practices?

➤ Please, tell me why is racism, hatred, and bigotry still realities in this nation although we have abolished American Chattel Slavery.

➤ Alcohol-related deaths take more lives than drug additions, so why is one legal and the other illegal?

➤ Multiple ministries, including broadcasts, telecasts, and outreach ministries are launched from our congregations, but look around and tell me what you see in our communities.

➤ Why is it we are having the discussion on gay rights and why was a bill passed to allow gays to openly serve in the military? Why is the term *rights* attached to this discussion?

➤ Discrimination in any form is inappropriate, but do we equate the struggle of gays and lesbians with the struggle of African Americans in this country?

➤ What has happened to our music in that profanity, disrespect, sexuality, and violence have become the norm to topping the chart?

➤ Where is the quality of life in our community? Dr. Howard Thurman once said, "At the core of life is a hard purposefulness, a determination to live."

➤ Do you fight for your faith, or do you succumb to

tradition and the status quo?

➢ Why are our public schools failing in record numbers, and why is the educational system in the USA lagging behind other nations?

➢ False teachers, images, concepts, idolatry, corruption, and a lack of understanding holiness, love, and faith have caused you to be where you are, spiritually speaking.

➢ What is a pillar? In the Old Testament, we observe the Hebrew term *Massebah* refers to a pillar, monument, memorial, or sacred stone. The New Testament Greek term *Stulos* has to do with a column supporting the weight of a building.

➢ Generally speaking, a pillar represents something of strength, undergirding, stability, or significant.

VI. Proposition

Have you ever entered a building after a tornado, hurricane, or other natural disaster struck and noticed the columns or pillars were damaged thus causing the building to sway or even fall? Have you gone to a church or an individual that you once reverenced and respected, but now you see them in a weakened state of being? Have you observed yourself falling away from the things that once gave you spiritual strength? If your answer is "yes" to any of these, then you really need to pay attention to what I am about to say, by means of highlighting the three pillars of the Church, so that hereafter you will be able to withstand any damage i.e. earth, air, fire and water.

VII. Body Points

1. Now, the first perspective I want you to take note of has to do with understanding **Holiness,** once and for all, as the nature of God and the way of life ordained for a true believer. This is done by

humbling yourself and asking God to deliver your heart and soul from a damnable life of sin and shame, so that an eternal foundation might be established for this present age and the one to come.

Holiness is much more than a denomination, concept, cliché, or ideology. Holiness (Qados) denotes being reverent, hallowed, separated, and devoted for sacred and spiritual use. God delights in the person and community who sanctifies for the sole use of worshipping and serving Him.

2. The second perspective has to do with fully understanding *love* is the single most important attribute or principle (motivational) of the Most High God in terms of viewing it as a strong, voluntary attachment to and desire for someone else thus unlocking the mystery of a relationship. This should cause each of you to pause and appreciate all the wonderful things God has and is doing on your behalf.

   Love is an endless energy because it emanates from a spiritual source. Love is grounded in sacrifice and action. Love epitomizes kindness and patience regardless of the circumstances surrounding it. Love is eternal, and it is designed to encourage and instruct you at the most opportune time.

3. Thirdly, I want you to understand and appreciate the final pillar of *faith* as an essential tool you must have in order to ignite a relationship with a holy and loving God. This means faith (Arnan & Pistis) expects certainty, ferocity, firmness, enduring, trust, and belief from us regardless of the circumstances. Faith uniquely allows the visible and invisible merge and creates spiritual rewards that are simply amazing as a result.

Faith in God allows a relationship to be ignited, constructed, and expanded, daily. Faith is an assurance God has your best interest at all times. Faith propels you through the challenges thus making you a better person. Faith seems to be tailor made for adversity and challenges.

VIII. Conclusion

In this sermon, I have tried to demonstrate like Jude there will always be scoffers and distractions in the faith community. I urged you to fully grasp the eternal meaning and purpose of holiness, love, and faith because they will enable you to live a fulfilled life in this world and the one to come. You must transcend religions, ideologies, and traditions to allow the Holy Spirit to govern your lives.

IX. Story

Let me close with this little story told by a Military Chaplain:

A soldier's little girl, whose father was being moved to a distant post, was sitting at the airport among her family's meager belongings. The girl was sleepy. She leaned against the packs and duffel bags. A lady came by, stopped, and patted her on the head.

"Poor child," she said, "You haven't got a home."

The child looked up in a surprise.

"But we do have a home," she said. "We just don't have a house to put it in."

Each of you may live in a house: your body, but where is your soul (home) being lodged? Allow the pillars of holiness, love, and faith to undergird you, and there will always be a home to dwell in no matter where you are. God bless.

35

Subject: What Really Happened on That Day?
Or
When it's Time to Make a Statement!
Text: Mark 11:1-11 4/l/12 & 4/13/14

Introduction

Story - Judge Ruling: Atheist and April Fool's Day

 The Prosecutor objected to the defendant about the holidays Easter and Passover because atheists had no holiday to celebrate. The judge dismissed the case and says, "The Atheists have a holiday: April 1st, April Fool's Day."

- The Gospel According to Mark is a Synoptic Gospel but also discloses unique characteristics such as the suffering servant, secret motif, Son of God, Son of Man, and Kingdom of God.
- The history and traditions of Palm Sunday (beginning in 4th century A.D., Spain)
- What are Passion Week and The Passover?
- The political climate in Jerusalem
- The social conditions in Jerusalem
- The religious realities in Jerusalem

The journey through life is designed to teach and cause maturity as opposed to punishing you. There comes a time when the truth will have to stand up inside of you and express itself in wholesome examples. This path can reveal both negative and positive occurrences. For instance, athletes declaring they are gay and lesbian; Tea Party & Conservatives' disdain for President Obama; and my profound love for spiritual concerns and Blacks, globally etc.

Problem: *It appears to me far too many of you have lost sight of what really happened on the day that kicks off the tradition known as Holy Week, in terms of people to people appearing to delight in gathering, making noise, waving, and putting things down as loyal followers, due to their failure to fully grasp the essence of the Christ-Event and what really happened on that day.*

36

- Jesus and the disciples stopped at the twin cities, Beth phage and Bethany (House of un-ripe figs), and disclosed a strategy for entering Jerusalem. This location was familiar to Jesus and the disciples.
- Each Gospel account gives us a perspective of this event with variations.
- It explains the significance of Mount of Olive: Old and New Testaments (burial grounds)
- Two disciples were sent to retrieve a colt/donkey, to borrow for a spiritual purpose.
- The realities Jesus foretold were witnessed just like He said.
- It explains the significance of the young colt in relation to Jesus (King of Peace).
- It identifies the expectations of the people as He entered Jerusalem.
- Religious leaders had distorted the true, eternal, and liberating message of the kingdom.
- Israel was currently a vassal state under Roman occupation.
- It conveys the significance of entering Jerusalem (truth and judgment), capital city.
- Jesus of History and Christ of Faith is expressed on that day.
- Cloaks and leafy branches were placed along the road.
- It tells why we shout "Hosanna! Blessed is he who comes in the name of the Lord!"
- What is triumphant with this scene can only be understood with the spiritual eye and not the temporal eye.
- Upon entering Jerusalem, He went to the temple (central place of worship), made an assessment, and returned to Bethany.
- What really happens when Jesus appears on the scene?
- What did the people know versus the religious and political leaders?

- Why was there so much animosity against Jesus and a plot to kill him?
- Know who you are and utilize the crowd without getting caught up with the hype.
- Jesus' appearance served as a pronouncement of judgment against the unrighteous and an array of hope for the disinherited.

Story - A Pastor was pulled over for speeding with passing motorists blowing their horns. Finally, the officer asked the driver what is going on. "I am the pastor of the church ahead, and these are members who recognized me." The officer smiled and tore up the ticket. "I think you have paid your debt to society," he said.

Contemporary Realities

- What is it about the Trayvon Martin case in Sanford, FL that has mobilized people?
- What really happened on the night of his murder?
- Where is the alarm when it comes to thousands of Blacks being killed every week?
- What is really going on with the random violence in the schools and military bases?
- What is at stake with voting, and why is there so much apathy, especially at primary?
- What is at stake with the Obamacare and Affordable Health Care Act? It is legally passed, but attempts are constantly made to repeal it, despite nearly 8 million already registered.
- Are you noticing the attention drawn to heroin addiction versus crack cocaine?
- Each of you must learn from Jesus and arrive at a day when you come out and let the world know who you are and what you stand for.
- Racial, economic, political, and religious realities will cause you to stand up and be heard or sit down and be trampled.

- For what cause or purpose are you standing for, or for what purpose or cause are you sitting down and remaining silent?
- God has a unique way of anointing and selecting men and women to provide leadership, so do not get stuck with traditions or the status quo.
- Do you fully understand the dynamic realities associated with ushering the Kingdom of God and Christ's triumphant entry?

Proposition- Have you ever gone along with the crowd or public opinion for the sake of doing so? However, you eventually found out what was truly going on and the person and public opinions did not represent the truth. This eye-opening moment or moment of awareness opened your eyes and caused you to make a change in direction. Therefore, since no one enjoys being deceived or misguided in terms of thinking it is one thing but in reality it is another, so let me share three perspectives you must consider regarding what really happened on that day.

Body

1. There comes a time when we must dramatize or amplify the mission or purpose assigned our hands to do, by means of doing precise things to show the status quo you are not intimidated or afraid of them, due to this will build your faith and help you truly understand what really happened on that day.
2. Secondly, each of you must participate in activities based upon knowledge and the truth (not mere emotions) you have personally discovered, in terms of allowing your praise and worship of Christ be an extension of the Word of God lodged in your heart and soul, simply because there is no greater reality that a man and woman living out their faith while appreciating what really happened on that day.
3. Thirdly, you must position yourself to understand and appreciate the dynamic realities   surrounding

39

mystery and truth, in terms of recognizing all physical expressions have a spiritual and eternal message beneath the surface, all because God has designed these methods to weed out who is faithful and unfaithful when it comes to what really happened on that day.

Conclusion

Story - Once, there was a millionaire who collected live alligators. He kept them in the pool behind his mansion. The millionaire also had a beautiful daughter who was single. One day, he decides to throw a huge party, and during the party announces "My dear guests... I have a proposition to the man who can swim across this pool full of alligators and emerge alive!"

As soon as he finished his last word, there was the sound of a large splash!! There was one guy in the pool swimming with all of his might and screaming to the top of his lungs. The crowd cheered him on as he kept stroking as though he were running for his life. Finally, he made it to the other side with only a torn shirt and some minor injuries. The millionaire was impressed.

He said, "My boy, that was incredible! Fantastic! I didn't think it could be done! Well I must keep my end of the bargain. Do you want my daughter or the one million dollars?"

The guys says, "Listen, I don't want your money, nor do I want your daughter! I want the person who pushed me in that water!"

Whether you are pushed, convinced, or deliberate, it is time to join Jesus as He triumphs through the nations. Jesus knew fully well what He was doing, and likewise, you may not like the push.

Nevertheless, we need to get busy and stop playing around. Seize the moment, but let it be for a righteous cause. If you must utilize *Prime Time,* then let it be for a cause that will make a difference.

I. **Subject: Demonstrations of Faith and
Deliverance (Part 1)**
II. **Text: 2 Kings 4ᵗʰ Chapter**
12/7/08; 1/2/11; 9/6/15; 1/31/16

III. Introduction

This message permeates around the life and
legacy of the esteemed prophet, Elisha (God saves)
and will be delivered in four sermons. There will
always be vexing situations throughout life, but you
will also explore profound lessons or solutions to
learn, therein. Elisha was successful and profound in
what he did simply because he was anointed and
fulfilled a purpose. Furthermore, he sat at the feet of
his esteemed mentor/spiritual advisor/teacher, Elijah
(The Lord, He is God). This illustration of a tandem
is consistently enacted throughout the Old and New
Testament. Effective leaders usually sit at the feet of
distinguished leaders.

We are about to get acquainted with the social,
political, economic and spiritual environment of
Israel during a period, wherein every king of the
Northern Kingdom (Israel) displeased Yahweh. At
the same time however, some of the kings of the
Southern Kingdom (Judah) had favorable
administrations.

Story - Joint Effort

Two moving men were struggling with a big
crate in a doorway. They pushed and tugged until
they were exhausted, but it would not move. Finally,
the man on the outside said, "We'd better give up,
because we'll never get this in." The fellow on the
inside said, "What do you mean get in, I thought you
were trying to get it out."

42

Background on the Book of Kings

- Both I & II Kings describe activities of the monarchy in Israel (ca. 970-586 B.C.)
- The kingdom was established or summoned by God and was destined to exemplify holiness and righteousness via the model illustrated by King David. However, in many instances, we see the influence of idolatry and corruption due to her relationship with various groups in Canaan.
- There is no single author; however, we believe the writings are the result of biblical scholars known as the *Deuteron mists* who emphasized righteous living (Dt. 4:29).
- The suggested date of compilation could be during and after the Babylonian Captivity.
- Key Themes: Yahweh is the only true God; Yahweh controls history; Yahweh demands exclusive worship; The content and place of true worship; The consequences of false worship; Yahweh as the just and gracious Lawgiver & Yahweh as the promise-giver.

Problem

It appears to me an alarming number of people are journeying through life without ever developing a wholesome relationship with the Most High God, by means of succumbing or giving in to the perplexing and annoying circumstances that frequently invade his or her life, due to a failure on your part of understanding the awesome relationship between your faith and the deliverance of our God.

Smaller Context and Outline of II Kings Chapter 4:1-44

➢ Elisha and the Widow's Oil (vs. 1-7)

➢ Elisha and the Shunammite Woman (vs. 8-17)

➢ Elisha Raises the Shunammite's Son (vs. 18-37)

➢ Elisha Purifies the Deadly Stew (vs. 38-42)

➢ Elisha and the Bread of the First-fruit (vs. 42-44)

Elisha and the Widow's Oil (Part 1)

Facts and Realities surrounding this story

➢ Death invaded the household of a Saint (un-named) who was also a member of the *Sons of the Prophets.*

➢ The sudden demise of her husband, a prophet and head of the household, created a void in the family and a series of challenges. She also had two sons, which complicates matters.

➢ Historically, creditors can be notorious when collecting debts; they could legally confiscate property, animals, and enslave family members to settle a debt.

➢ Elisha is following a pattern similar to his mentor, Elijah, by going place to place in order to bring glory to God.

➢ The prophet (Nabi or seer) declared the oracles of God; proclaimed a message of righteousness as well as foretold futuristic events.

- Whenever the righteous face a situation or problem, God delights in putting forth a question(s) in order to examine your spiritual state of being. Being fully aware of the grave reality at hand, Elisha asked, "What shall I do for you?"

- The widow is so pre-engaged in her realities; she ignored or dismissed the question.

- The prophet could not be caught up in her world of emotion, frustration, and anxiety; therefore, he simply set forth another question in order to shift her attention from the distasteful reality of worrying to the reality of change (potentiality). He went on to ask "What have you in your house?"

- In order for God to deliver her or you from troubles or situations, there must be some participation; whereby, you become aware that you always have something to work with.

- She unenthusiastically replied, "Your servant has nothing in the house *except* a jar of oil." Prior to the dialog, she was unaware or never thought about the value of a jar on hand. He was sent there to help make a difference, and we see it unfold.

- The oil is used in this scenario because it has metaphorical significance in scripture i.e., spirit, anointing, and deliverance. Remember, the source of the oil can never run out.

- She may have been a little apprehensive or reluctant, but nonetheless, she cooperated with the Man of God's instructions.

- He instructs her to do something, which on the surface makes no sense. She is instructed to go and *borrow* as many vessels as possible from her neighbors. Remember, she is already broke and indebted. Trust me, when you are *down and out,* more than likely, nobody seems to want to help. It is something like an unemployed person trying to borrow money from the bank without collateral. It is highly unlikely.

➢ "Faith is to believe in that which you cannot see and the reward of faith is to see that which you believe" (St Augustine).

➢ Remember, you can always do something, so do not quit. "When things go wrong, as they sometimes will; when the road you're trudging seems all uphill; when the funds are low and the debts are high, and you want to smile, but you have to sigh; when care is pressing you down a bit, rest, if you must-but don't quit. It's when things seem worst you must not quit." (Anonymous)

➢ Upon fulfilling the assignment, both the widow and her sons were instructed to **withdraw** (shut the door) from the public.

➢ Now, watch the miracle unfold. They started with a single jar of oil (it starts with you), but the blessed oil overflowed as they poured it into a container, and so did the next and next and next. This continued until every vessel they had borrowed (we are all on borrowed time) and carried into the room was full. We do not know how many containers were borrowed, but here is a clear reminder for each of you to allow your faith to keep growing.

➢ They eventually ran out of vessels, but never the oil. Likewise, you cannot exhaust the spirit of holiness, love and faith. However, the oil always needs containers and once all the containers were filled, the oil stopped flowing. The Lord will work with that which you offer, but it will not be spilled and wasted.

> Now, the widow saw a gradual and wholesome transformation in her situation due to the instruction from the prophet and equally important with her participation.

> She displayed responsibility by reporting to the man of God and telling him what happened, even though he already knew. What he told her would bring deliverance.

> She returned to Elisha, and he instructs her to go sell the oil and pay the debts. Simultaneously, there was oil left over to sustain the household for an extended period.

> Do you truly understand faith? It reminds me of a little story about a storm raging on the sea. When the captain realized the ship was sinking fast, he called out "Anyone know how to pray?" One man stepped forward. "Aye, captain, I know how to pray." The captain said, "You pray while the rest of us put on our life jackets. We are one short."

Contemporary Realities

> The global economy is faced with financial (not wealth) challenges due to poor management and greed that is causing both the rich and poor to make adjustments.

> There are strange weather patterns displayed in the world.

> There are Heads of State determined to hold onto political power even at the expense of

47

massive suffering such as we observe in Europe, Asia, Africa, South and North America.

➢ President Obama heads the executive branch of government in the USA as a visionary leader; however, Congress, during his administration, opposes him far too often.

➢ There are health epidemics all over the world that can be eliminated, but token gestures are being done to address these grave conditions.

➢ Murders and homicides have reached epidemic proportion on multiple fronts.

➢ Abortions head the list of deaths in the USA, especially African Americans, but why is this information suppressed and where is the open outrage?

➢ The African American Community has shown great resilience despite the psychological scars of American Chattel Slavery. However, we are faced with new realities i.e. children forced to be raised by grandparents and parents with poor values. In addition, where are the men in the homes and community? Where have they gone?

➢ We do not know the cause of the prophet's death in our story, but this interruption created a problem and so it is in our community.

➢ On the surface, millions of jobs are being lost, but what do you suppose would happen if all the banking, auto, Wall Street, media, entertaining, and athletic executives, etc. came together and donated twenty billion dollars into the underprivileged communities that are directly impacted? This gesture alone would boost the morale of the people and create an atmosphere for wholesome recovery. Even in bad times, we must show creativity and cooperation versus looking for a hand out.

➤ What is a miracle? Scripturally, the term derives from the Greek words *dunamis* which denotes power and inherent ability. It occurs through acts of supernatural origin and character, such as those things that are not produced by natural agents or means. The N.T. term *semeion* refers to a sign, mark, or token; a means of displaying spiritual authority within the human drama. They only occur when it is necessary, but wisdom is always available.

➤ Miracles are strategically placed throughout the world; wherein, a righteous person is utilized in order to assist God in demonstrating His awesome power in a distasteful situation, while at the same time, igniting faith among the observers. Miracles are instruments of change and barometers of inspiration along life's journey.

IV.   Proposition

Since no one in his or her right mind delights in embarrassment such as being harassed by your creditors or having to borrow and beg for survival, our text suggests three things you need to do, so that you too will learn from the life and legacy of Elisha regarding profound demonstrations of faith and deliverance.

V.   Body

1. Now, the first thing you need to do is position yourself to get a handle on the situation or interruptions that have altered your lifestyle. This is done by humbling yourself to be quiet and hear what the spirit of truth is saying directly or indirectly about your situation.   This

will help to establish a foundation of trust and confidence in God regarding Demonstrations of Faith and Deliverance.

2. Secondly, you need to get a firm handle regarding biblical and spiritual meanings of faith in terms of actively participating in a life of faith in God such as being certain, enduring, grounded in righteousness and truthful etc., despite the physical circumstances surrounding you. All of these experiences were designed to build faithful character that is molded after the same spirit of Elisha-Demonstrations of Faith and Deliverance.

3. The third thing you need to do is understand God is always in control although He allows distasteful realities to occur in order to ultimately bring forth deliverance, and knowing without a shadow of doubt, it is available for the righteous come arrest and place those things that hindered your spiritual mobility, so that you realize God takes pleasure and delight in liberating you from things having the capability of annoying and destroying you-Demonstrations of Faith and Deliverance.

VI.   Conclusion & Story

We have embarked upon a four-part sermon surrounding a man of faith and several un-named characters during a time of corruption, idolatry, and an impoverished condition. Nonetheless, Elisha like Elijah adhered to the voice of the Most High God, and not only was he blessed, but all those who listened and adhered were blessed as well. The next sermon will show diversity transitioning from a poor widow to a wealthy woman, but she too needed the man of God to intervene on her behalf.

I would like to close with this story entitled, *Just One Question.* A teacher, garbage collector, and lawyer wound up together at the Pearly Gates. St. Peter informed each of them they would have to answer one question in order to get into Heaven.

St. Peter addressed the teacher and asked, "What was the name of the ship that crashed into the iceberg? They just made a movie about it." The teacher answered quickly, "That would be the Titanic." St. Peter let him through the gate.

St. Peter turned to the garbage man and figuring Heaven did not really need all the odors this guy would bring with him, decided to make the question a little harder: "How many people died on the ship?" Fortunately for him, the trash man had just seen the movie and answered, "About 1500."

"That's right! You may enter."

St. Peter turned to the lawyer and said, "Name them."

If you want a favorable journey and successful ending embrace humility and do not display the character of arrogance like the lawyer in our story. Instead, follow the Lord's instruction via the man or woman of God.

Alternative Story

Let me end with the wonderful and eye-opening story entitled: *The Woman with the Fork*. A young woman was diagnosed with a terminal illness and given three months to live. She wanted to get everything in order; therefore, she called her Pastor to her home to discuss certain aspects of her final wishes.

She told him the songs, scriptures, and outfit for her burial. Eventually, he prepared to leave, and she suddenly remembered something very important: "One more thing," she said "What's that?" replied the Pastor. She said, "It is very important: I want to be buried with a fork in my right hand." The Pastor was amazed and puzzled at this request. "That surprises you, doesn't it?" said the young woman.

"Yes." She went on to explain. "My grandmother once told me this story, and I have passed it along to those I love and need encouragement. In all my years of socials and dinners, I have always remembered someone would lean over and say '*keep your fork*' when the dishes of the main course were being cleared. It was a favorite part i.e. chocolate cake, deep-dish pie etc. Something wonderful!

"So, I just want people to see me in that casket with a fork, and I do want them to wonder, *what's with the fork?* Then, I want you to tell them, 'Keep the fork because the best and most delightful part of the meal is yet to come."

Pastor's eyes welled up with tears of joy as he hugged her and said good-bye while reflecting on the great maturity and focus of this young woman.

At the funeral, people walked by the casket and saw the cloak she wore and the fork in her right hand. Repeatedly the Pastor heard, *"What's with the fork?"* In addition, he smiled. In his sermon, he explained, 'The next time you reach for a fork that is left behind, remind yourself the best is yet to come. In addition, the next time you encounter troubles and trials like the widow in our sermon, just remember you are in the proximity for a miracle. In addition, oh do not forget the fork because it is a reminder God has something delightful at the end. Keep your Fork!"

Demonstrations of Faith and Deliverance (Part 2)

2 Kings 4:8-17
12/14/08; 1/9/11; 5/15/13

Introduction

In the previous sermon, I introduced the distinguished prophet, Elisha (God saves). He was a faithful student and mentee of the legendary prophet, Elijah (The Lord, He is God). Prophets played a significant role in the life of Israel or the covenant community because they were anointed servants of God summoned to proclaim a message of righteousness, stir the hearts of the people, and alert them about futuristic events at the same time. Once again, we are about to discover the faith and passion Elisha had for God and the consistent manner God ushered in deliverance through him.

Story - The Atheist Holy Day

In Florida, an atheist created a case against the upcoming Easter and Passover holy days. He hired an attorney to bring a discrimination case against Christians and Jews for observances of their holy days. The argument was that it was unfair and atheists had no such recognized day.

The case was brought before a judge. After listening to the passionate presentation by the lawyer, the judge banged his gavel and declared, "Case dismissed."

The lawyer immediately stood and objected to the ruling and said "Your Honor, how can you possibly dismiss this case? The Christians have Christmas, Easter, and others. The Jews have Passover, Yom Kippur, and Hanukkah. Yet my client and all other atheists have no such holidays."

The judge leaned forward in his chair and said, "But you do. Your client, counsel, is woefully ignorant of the facts."

The lawyer said, "Your Honor, we are unaware of any special observance or holiday for atheists."

The judge said, "The calendar says April 1st is April fool's Day. Psalms 14:1 states, 'The fool has said in his heart there is no God.' Therefore, it is the opinion of this court that if your client says there is no God, then he is a fool. Therefore, April 1st is his day. Court is dismissed."

Background on the Book of Kings

In the previous sermon, we shared general information regarding Yahweh's desire to present Israel as a holy and model nation. She was summoned and expected to exemplify holiness, love, and faith. Once again, the key themes permeated around Yahweh controlling history, demanding exclusive worship. Other themes are centered upon the content, place of true worship, and the consequences of false worship. They also discuss Yahweh as a just and gracious Lawgiver (as a promise-giver).

Problem

It appears to me a disproportionate number of people are tracking through life without fully discovering his or her Creator and their mission in life, eliminate in this aspect by means of this seems to stem from always yielding to those challenging and disheartening situations that come across their path, simply because Satan has created a serious, spiritual disconnection in the role of faith and deliverance.

Facts and realities surrounding this story

➤ According to the land allotment for the Children of Israel, Shunem was situated among the Tribe of Issachar in Northern Israel.

➤ By contrast in the last sermon, we were introduced to a widow with meager means in debt and distressed. However, in this sermon, we will become acquainted with a woman who was blessed with resources. Godliness in character is often hidden in humility just like we see in this un-named woman and the previous widow.

➤ Once again, we observe the mobility and diverse interactions encountered by the man of God throughout Israel.

➤ The family is introduced showing hospitality and kindness toward the messenger of God. Additionally, it appears he visited this family, quite often.

➤ Elisha's demeanor and character as a prophet was admirable, honorable, and welcoming to the extent that she asked her husband if it would be all right to add a private room to the house for him to lodge. More than likely, this room was placed on the flat roof in a secluded area. The room consisted of a bed, table, chair, and lamp.

➢ This family loved and trusted the man of God and wanted to accommodate him whenever he passed through their area.

➢ As time passed, Elisha returned to the home in Shunem along with his assistant/servant, Gehazi. However, upon this visit, he felt led to do something special on her behalf. This reminds me of an African proverb that says, "Being grateful, a man makes himself deserving of yet another kindness."

➢ Elisha instructs Gehazi to call the Shunammite, and she came to Elisha's chamber.

➢ In the previous message, I emphasized there must be questions and participation targeted to those in need if they truly want to experience deliverance.

➢ We observe the coming together of culture and religious protocol in verse 13, because Elisha channels the conversation through Gehazi even though she is before him.

➢ This story is also unusual because of the attention given to this woman while her husband remains in the background. This has spiritual significance because today far too many men are in the background spiritually, yet they want to lay claim to being the head of the family.

➢ Elisha is grateful for this room, meals, and acts of kindness; therefore, he makes the following inquiries: What can I do for you? Would you like me to speak a favorable word to the King or to the commander of the army? Elijah is unlike his predecessor because he had a favorable relationship with the King.

➢ In this instance, Elisha ministers before the King of Judah, Jehoshaphat, and King of Israel, Jehoram (son of Ahab). Shunem was located in Israel.

- Unlike the widow in the previous sermon, she replied, "I dwell among my own people." In other words, I am doing just fine and there seem to be no apparent need. She felt secure with a husband, clan, property, and sources of income because she was described as a wealthy woman. In the previous story, the widow was vulnerable, but she was content and secure in this instance.

- Despite her impressive remarks and status, the man of God was determined to do something on her behalf. She asked for nothing because she was content in giving and serving on behalf of the man of God.

- Elisha consulted with Gehazi by asking the last question to him. "What then is to be done for her?" He replied, "Well, she has no son, and her husband is old." This can imply she had daughters or she was barren. I find it to be interesting the Bible seems to associate blessings with the birth of a son because the potential for growth and expansion in the family is located there.

- She came to the prophet's room as if to say she had departed after the earlier questions (vs. 12-13).

- This time, Elisha does not ask any questions. Instead, he makes a decree on behalf of the Most High God to a gracious and humble woman. As you can see, prophets cannot only declare oracles of doom and judgment because they can also pronounce blessings.

- In light of her radiant spirit and example of righteousness, He said, "At this season, about this time next year, you shall embrace a son." This epitomized what I understand to be the nature of a gift: unsolicited, unmerited, and full of surprises.

- Listen to her response: "No my lord, O man of God; do not lie to your servant."

- ➢ Now, we come to understand why Elisha and Gehazi did what they did. God wanted to expose to her because there was another level of faith and spirituality. In other words, she was content serving like many women during her era, and obviously, she had become comfortable with her situation.
- ➢ Just like the man of God had spoken, she became pregnant and gave birth to a son in the spring (Nisan/Abib).

Now, we all love a successful conclusion like we see in this story, but I will introduce both the blessings of the child to the family as well as the tragedy (interruption) that occurred with the child in the next sermon. Therefore, Elisha will have to help and instruct her in the school of faith and deliverance, once again.

Contemporary realities

- ➢ Where has the spirit of humility and hospitality gone among the wealthy in this world in comparison to this wealthy Shunammite woman?
- ➢ What are the bankers, automakers, Wall Street brokers, athletes, entertainers, and politicians really doing to help people in dire need?
- ➢ Why do we neglect to invite the traveling evangelist/preachers into our homes instead of always placing them in hotels, anymore?
- ➢ Where is the spirit of contentment and gratitude in what God has given you?
- ➢ Where is the reverence for the Word of God and His messengers, or can you truly recognize those whom God has called and anointed?
- ➢ The financial crisis in the USA can be corrected if we tighten our belts, make some sacrifices, and better organize our efforts.

- Wealth has several unique purposes, *Spend, Save, Invest, and Give* because, therein, lies a holistic approach to living.
- Annually, Muslims, Jews, and Christians turn inward to worship and celebrate i.e. El Hajj, Hanukkah, and Christmas because there seems to be a turning or inclination toward giving during the month of December.
- Occasionally, you appear to have everything until God uses a unique way of sending someone to teach you something new or enlighten you about another level of spirituality.
- What are you doing to go out of your way to make someone else comfortable?
- Why is the husband so silent in the household? Could it be he was so involved in wealth and riches until he forgot what it meant to praise and worship God?
- Where are the men when it comes to spiritual matters and receiving the man/woman of God as they pass through?
- This couple seems to have everything, but they failed to have what could bring true happiness i.e. a son.
- What is wealth? Scripturally, the Old Testament Hebrew term *Hon* refers to substance, riches, possession, enough, or abundance. Wealth is earned through hard work, inheritance, acquisition through ungodly measures, and blessings from the Lord.
- How did you get what you have, and what are you doing with it?
- Let us recap what the widow had going on prior to receiving and doing what she did for the man of God. She was wealthy, comfortable, mature, compassionate, hospitable, contented, married, and respected in her community but had no son.

Proposition

I wonder how many of you are truly content with the lot God has assigned your hands at this juncture in life while understanding kindness always has a unique way of getting the Lord's attention, causing Him to act or move on your behalf because you need to fully understand the role of faith and deliverance. Therefore, our text suggests three perspectives you should consider since all of us like to keep expanding and being creative, so these experiences will strengthen your faith and cause deliverance.

Body

1. Now, the first perspective hinges upon positioning yourself to obtain a firmer grasp of the biblical principle of *giving* by means of viewing this virtue as a form of ministry, deliverance, sacrificing, kindness, granting, rendering, and showing hospitality on behalf of another without any strings attached. This is because godly behavior will help establish or usher you in the arena or proximity of God's favor.

2. Secondly, you need to open your heart and soul to the biblical principle of *contentment* in a world that is driven by greed and need and view this attribute as a spiritual state of being passed on to you in order to be an example of righteousness: sufficient, enough, and being able. This will enable you to navigate through life a whole lot easier, knowing fully well that this demeanor pleases God.

3. Thirdly and finally, you need to really understand the biblical meaning of *deliverance* in a world where so many are living in bondage in that this virtue is a characteristic of God

extended to the saints in the form of rescuing, setting free, placing under custody, and restoring to a rightful place. God allows awkward situations to occur in order for faith to be ignited and miracles to be performed.

Conclusion & Story

In this second sermon, I have shared with you the manner in which the man of God was mobile and utilized by God. This mobility caused him to ignite faith and deliverance in a world surrounded with idolatry and distorted views of the truth. We moved from a widow in distress to a content, wealthy woman living a good life with her husband. Her acts of kindness resulted in the pronouncement of a blessing: a son. Despite her admirable lifestyle, we detected doubt and skepticism when the man of God shared this with her. Nonetheless, the child will come as promised, but in the next sermon, we will articulate how blessings are usually met with challenges and obstacles.

All of us have needs even though they are often hidden like this wealthy woman. Make sure each of you is connected to what the Word has to say. Let me close with the story about a new pastor. Anxious about delivering his first sermon, the new preacher had gotten little sleep throughout the week before he was to address his church. By Sunday morning, he was both exhausted and extremely nervous. Nevertheless, he managed to make it up the few steps onto the platform. He had barely begun his presentation when everything he had planned to say flew right out of his mind. In fact, his mind went totally blank. Then, he remembered seminary had taught him what to do if a situation as this ever arose: "Repeat your last point, and let it remind you what is coming next."

Figuring this advice could not hurt, he recalled the last thing he'd said and repeated it. "Behold," he quoted, "I come quickly." His mind was still blank. He thought he had better try it, again. "Behold, I come quickly." Still nothing! He tried it one more time, but in his panic, he pronounced the words with such force that he lost his balance, fell forward, knocked the pulpit to one side, tripped over a flower arrangement, and fell into the lap of a little old woman in the front row.

Flustered and embarrassed, he picked himself up, apologized profusely, and started to explain what had just happened. "Oh, that's all right Preacher" said the woman, kindly. "It was my fault, really. You told me three times you were coming, quickly. I should have gotten out of your way!"

Alternative Story

Every year, our nation observes Mental Health Week; therefore, I thought I would share this little conversation.

"Hello. Thanks for calling the State Mental Health Hospital. Please, select from the following options on the menu:
'If you are *obsessive-compulsive*, please press 1 repeatedly.'
'If you are *co-dependent*, please ask someone to press 2 for you.'
'If you have *multiple personalities*; press 3, 4, 5, & 6.'
'If you are *paranoid,* we know who you are and what you want, stay on the line, so we can trace your call.'
'If you are *delusional,* press 7 and all your calls will be forwarded to the Mother ship.'
'If you are *schizophrenic*, listen carefully and a little voice will tell you which number to press.'

'If you are *manic-depressive*, hang up. It does not matter which number you press.'

'Nothing will make you happy, anyway.'

'If you are *dyslexic*, press 9-6-9-6.'

'If you are *bi-polar*, please leave a message after the beep or before the beep or after the beep. Please, wait for the beep.'

'If you have a *short term memory loss*, press 9.'

'If you have a *short term memory loss*, press 9.'

'If you have a *short term memory loss*, press 9.'

'If you have *low self-esteem*, please hang up because our operators are too busy to talk to you.'

'If you are *menopausal*, put the gun down, hang up, turn on the fan, lie down, and cry. You won't be crazy, forever.'

'If you are a *blonde*, don't press any button. You will just mess it up.'

All of us have issues and concerns; whereby, we need deliverance. Let us not get caught up with the stereotypes. You may think all is well, but God has sent me to ask the question "What can He do for you?" If you take time and reflect on this question, you just might find yourself getting His attention. Alternatively, if you do not answer the question, just maybe He will linger around and bless you anyhow because you have been showing kindness to others. God bless!

Demonstrations of Faith and Deliverance (Part 3)
2 Kings 4:18-37
12/28/08; 5/16/13; 3/6/16

Introduction

In the previous sermons, we introduced the anointed prophet, Elisha (God saves). In addition, we were told he was mentored by the esteemed prophet, Elijah (The Lord is God). Please remember, prophets served as an essential spiritual agent within the covenant community alongside the priest and king. In order for the prophet to be effective, he or she must declare the oracles of God, uncompromisingly. I want to go a little further in this chapter and expound upon a new challenge that will ultimately result in deliverance.

Story - The Carrot, the Egg, and the Coffee

A young woman went to her mother and told her about her life and how things were going so hard for her. She did not know how she was going to make it and wanted to give up; she was tired of struggling. It seemed a new problem arose as soon as one was solved. Her mother took her to the kitchen. She filled three pots with water and placed each on high fire. Soon the pots came to a boil. She placed carrots in the first. She placed eggs in the second. Coffee grounds were placed in the third. Then, she let them sit and boil without saying a word.

In about twenty minutes, she turned off the burners. She took the carrots out and placed them in a bowl. Next, she took the eggs out and placed them in a bowl. Then, she poured the coffee into a bowl. Turning to her daughter, she asked. "Tell me what you see."

"Carrots, eggs and coffee," she replied.

Her mother brought her closer and asked her to feel the carrots; she did and noted they were soft. Then, the mother asked the daughter to take an egg and break it. After pulling off the shell, she observed the hard-boiled egg.

Finally, the mother asked the daughter to sip the coffee. The daughter smiled as she tasted its rich aroma. The daughter then asked, "What does it mean, mother?" Stick around for the end of this sermon, and I will explain what it means.

Background on the book of Kings

Just in case you missed the earlier sermons in this series, let me reiterate the book of Kings. It gives us a spiritual and historical perspective of life and activities within the covenant community, Israel, during a period known as the United and Divided Kingdoms. The reign of King David served as the model monarchy or spiritual template because he represented the true meaning of praise and worship.

This sermon does not focus on the activities of the king per se. Instead, it is predicated upon the life and legacy of a prophet, Elisha. We will explore the righteousness of the Most High God and the role of faith in individuals demonstrating how to face and overcome adversities.

Problem

It seems to me there are many people going through life without ever making the ultimate connection with his or her mission in life, in that they display frailty and weakness when adversities strike, surprisingly, all because you allow the evil one (Satan) to take control over your spirit instead of knowing your faith can bring forth deliverance.

Facts and realities surrounding the story

> - In the previous story, we highlighted a void in this family, even though the woman was content as a giver and an example of hospitality.
> - Nonetheless, Elisha was inspired to pronounce a blessing upon her in the form of conception and birth of a son. The child became the center of attention in the household, even though the couple was wealthy, content, and advanced in age.
> - There are some things money cannot buy such as family and the state of happiness. The child grew, and at this juncture in the story, we assume he was several years old.
> - One day, the child experienced a serious headache (that eventually would be passed along

to him) while outdoors with his father overseeing the estate.

➤ The headache was excruciating, so it prompted the father to send him back to the house by one of the servants for his mother to take charge of their child's care. I guess some things do not change when it comes to traditional views of a father being able to attend to the needs of a child. Meanwhile, there is nothing like a mother's touch or care.

➤ The mother held him in her lap, praying and believing God for deliverance. Here, we see the grace, love, and care of a mother just as if we see it emanating from God toward us.

➤ The child died despite the mother's valiant effort. Bad things can and will happen to good people, including little children.

➤ Notice the response and attitudes of both the mother and father, even though both are equally sad.

➤ The Africans say "Children are the reward of life," and it leaves a tremendous void and emptiness one cannot explain when a child dies before their parents.

➤ It appears the father is willing to accept this painful reality or sudden death; however, the mother immediately thinks otherwise and refuses to accept this fate.

➤ The birth of the child was linked to the man of God, and she simply refused to let the story end like this. Therefore, she took the child, laid him upon the bed of the prophet (Elisha), and left him there. The woman, who was content but blessed with a son, is now behaving the way a faithful witness is supposed to behave in troublesome situations (retracing the steps).

➤ She was not done; therefore, she summoned her husband to instruct a servant to get the best donkey in order for them to go immediately and tell the man of God what has happened.

➤ The husband's response seemed to be grounded in traditional, religious beliefs because he made mention of the new moon and Sabbath. Alternatively, she is allowing her faith to pursue unconventional territories. Respect, understand, and preserve traditions, but do not become enslaved by them.

➤ Before she left home, it was resolved in her spirit this death was not permanent and said this to her husband: "It is well."

➤ Her mission had a sense of urgency; therefore, she tells the servant "Urge the animal on; do not slacken the pace for me unless I tell you." In other words, do not allow my age, gender, or condition to alter your assignment.

➤ Eventually, she arrived at Mt. Carmel (the place where earlier God used Elijah to transform it from the worship of Baal to the worship of the true and living God) because that is where the man of God was worshipping.

➤ Elisha managed to see her from a distance (attributes of a prophet) and said to Gehazi, his servant, "Behold, there is the Shunammite."

➤ In addition, he instructed Gehazi to run out to greet her and ask in a tri-fold greeting, "Is it well with you, your husband and child?"

➤ This form of greeting reminds me of a typical Senegalese greeting that goes something like this: *Nan ga def* (How are you)? *Ana wa quer ga* (How is the family)? *Nak ka yee tay* (How is the business)? *Nun ga fa* (All is well)!

➤ The woman responded to Gehazi, "It is well." The response and character of this woman is what fascinates and attracts me to her because it shows a lot about who she really was. As a matter of facts, I have incorporated this   phrase into my greetings for years by asking, "Is it well, or all is well?"

➢ She was able to say "it is well" because the man of God and her son's birth and death helped her reach a new level of faith and spirituality.

➢ When she reached the mountain where Elisha was located; she latched onto the feet of the prophet.

➢ Gehazi attempted to push her away as a gesture of loyalty and respect for the man of God, but Elisha stepped in and told him to leave her, alone.

➢ Here again, Elisha detected a need and is touched by her demeanor. He was able to discern this woman is in bitter distress, and God had hidden it from him.

➢ We must take note from these words and realize men and women of God must be sensitive to the needs of others while knowing only God is Omniscient. We only know and speak according to knowledge and revelation we receive. You do not know everything regardless of how many Spiritual Gifts you possess.

➢ Elisha allowed her to talk, and she reminded him she was content with what she was doing and what she already had as a family. Putting it another way, she let him have it by reminding Elisha he mentioned and declared she would have a child. Now, she feels deceived and mocked.

➢ Elisha allowed her to fully express herself and just as she was determined to see him. Then, Elisha was determined to see a successful conclusion to this story.

➢ Elisha instructs Gehazi to tie his garment in order to travel quickly to the place where the deceased child was laid.

➢ He is told not to greet or salute anyone along the way, and likewise, we should display the same discipline when we are on assignment for the Kingdom of God.

➤ Gehazi is under authority of the prophet, and he placed Elisha's staff upon the face of the deceased child upon arrival. A staff has been used symbolically as an extension of the anointing placed upon the individual in order to assist in ushering deliverance.

➤ The mother was pleased with this gesture, but she came for Elisha and was not leaving his presence until he returned with her.

➤ Gehazi went ahead and fulfilled his assignment, but there was no change in the child. In addition, he was returning to meet Elisha, and the Shunammite woman, and told them "the child has not awakened."

➤ Neither Elisha nor the woman is disturbed or discouraged by this report.

➤ Upon arrival at the house, Elijah entered his room alone and saw the child laying dead on the bed. How do you face adversities and situations that seem hopeless?

➤ Elisha does the following: lie upon the child, put his mouth on his mouth, eyes on his eyes, and hands upon his hand in an attempt to transpose or transfer life (Ruach Yahweh) from himself to the child.

➤ After a while, the child transitioned from cold to warm but was yet in a prostrate position.

➤ Elisha got up, walked around and repeated the same ritual. Rituals grounded in faith and a vibrant spirit will bring good results. The child continued to lie there, and this caused Elisha to do the same, again.

➤ Afterward, the child sneezed seven times (completion). Then, he opened his eyes.

➤ Elisha summoned Gehazi to call the Shunammite woman to observe what her faith had prompted God to do on her behalf.

- She saw her resurrected son upon entering the room, and Elisha instructed her: "Pick up your son."
- Afterward, she fell at the prophet's feet in a spirit of gratitude according to the custom of bowing to the ground. She then took her son and went out praising God.

Contemporary realities

- In the text, we saw a child die because of a severe headache. What is causing the death of our children before their parents? In many instances, it is alcohol, drugs, violence, dieting, recklessness, and depression.
- Why do we see a vast contrast in the way men and women respond when it comes to spiritual matters?
- Where is your focus and determination when it comes to overcoming adversities and fulfilling a spiritual mandate?
- Do you have a place called your *praying ground* in a manner similar to where Elisha was easily found?
- Are you able to allow someone in distress to vent out his or her frustration and then have the wherewithal to understand you do not know everything?
- Can you work through various challenges until you see the hands of God usher in deliverance?
- Do you have the patience and passion to do whatever it takes to see wholesome results take place?
- Can you keep working until you see the full resuscitation take place?

> Once God restores what has been interrupted, can you display reverence, gratitude, praise, and worship?

Proposition

Please be mindful, adversities will come in various forms and some will be deadly? For example, it appears the African American Community is dead. However, as Ambassadors of the Kingdom of God, we understand challenges come to make us strong and better, not bitter. Therefore, there are three distinct perspectives you need to consider since none of us wants to be labeled losers in life. Presently, you can also embrace the principles and practices of demonstrations of faith and deliverance.

Body

1. Now, the first perspective permeates around getting a firm grasp of **faith** from a Biblical standpoint in terms of viewing faith as the anchoring presence and building block of your relationship with God on a daily basis. Consequently, this will establish you as a true servant of God in a similar manner to the Shunammite woman in our sermon.

2. Secondly, we need to understand the role or various **methods** the Lord will allow such as we observed in the scripture. We clearly observed, in this instance, a life of faith caused Elisha to lay on the child, place himself hand to hand, eye to eye and mouth to mouth as a means of giving our all in all to the assignment at hand. Ultimately, this is because it will help you understand there is no quitting or failure when it

comes to the righteous allowing God to bring forth deliverance.

3. Thirdly, we really need to understand and appreciate the true meaning of **resurrection theology** in scripture because Elisha highlighted three senses i.e. hands, eyes, and mouth as well as laid upon the child three times until he saw the coming forth of the child from a deep sleep due to the woman and man of faith realizing life is greater than death.

Conclusion & Story

I have tried to emphasize the significant role of the prophet being a messenger of God while I wanted to show there are persons who will play a significant role in life without his or her names ever being mentioned. In addition, we demonstrated interruptions will occur and death does not discriminate regardless of the magnitude of one's happiness. However, joy is greater than sorrow, and life is greater than death when it is all said and done. We salute the legacy of Elisha and, most definitely, we applaud the humility and tenacity of the Shunammite Woman.

Now, let me conclude the story about the Carrots, Eggs, and Coffee. The daughter wanted to know the meaning of tasting and seeing the transformation of each. Her mother explained each of these objects had faced adversities: boiling water. Each reacted, differently. The carrots went in strong, hard, and unrelenting. However, they softened and became weak after being subjected to the boiling water. The egg had been fragile. Its thin outer shell had protected its liquid interior, but after sitting through the boiling water, its inside became hardened.

The ground beans were unique; however, they changed the water after they were in the boiling water. Think of this: Which am I? Am I the carrot that seems strong, but do I wilt and become soft and lose my strength with pain and adversity?
Am I the egg that starts with a malleable heart which changes after the heat? Did I begin with a fluid spirit that became hardened and stiff after a death, a breakup, a financial hardship, or some other trial? Does my shell look the same despite being bitter and tough with a stiff spirit and hardened heart?

Alternatively, am I like the coffee bean? The bean actually changes the hot water, the very circumstance that brings the pain... When the water gets hot, it releases the fragrance and flavor. If you are like the bean, when things are at their worst, you get better and change the situation around you. Do you elevate yourself to another level in the darkest hour when trials are at their greatest? How do you handle adversity? Are you a carrot, an egg, or a coffee bean?

May you have enough happiness to make yourself sweet, enough trials to make you strong, enough sorrow to keep you human, and enough hope to keep you happy. The happiest people do not necessarily have the best of everything; they just make the most of everything that comes along their way. The brightest future will always be based on a forgotten past; you cannot go forward in life until you let go of your past failures and headaches.

When you were born, you came forth crying with everyone around you smiling. Live your life, so you are the one who is smiling that at the end, even if everyone around you is crying. Thank God for yet another demonstration of faith and deliverance.

Demonstrations of Faith and Deliverance (Part 4)
2 Kings 4:38-44
1/11/09; 5/17/13; 1/24/16

Introduction

In the previous sermons (3), we introduced or presented the servant of God, Elisha (God saves). We also shared he was the mentee of one of the most heralded prophets of Israel, Elijah (The Lord is God).

Even further, we emphasized the importance of the prophets of Israel being spiritually mandated and anointed to represent the Most High God by proclaiming the oracles of God, the covenant community, and surrounding nations. In addition, prophets served alongside the priest and king thus giving us a trifold representation of righteousness within the kingdom.

Thus far, we have presented several stories involving Elisha as a spiritual enabler, assisting those in need within Israel. For example, we introduced him aiding a poor widow with her sons deeply emerged in debt to the extent they were about to be sold into slavery. Next, we observed him in Shunem interacting with a wealthy woman who was content serving the man of God. Nonetheless, he was led to pronounce the blessing of a son to the family, even though she asked for nothing. In the previous sermon, we saw the joy of a son in the family eventually give way to a premature death. Nonetheless, the

Shunammite woman's faith and tenacity resulted in prompting Elisha to pray for the restoration of her son.

This sermon will climax our series by highlighting a pair of wonderful and practical stories centered on food being provided in a desperate situation as a result of a famine. We will see the rebuking of death in the food that was provided as well as the scarcity of food resulting in a tremendous leftover. It has been said, "We cannot control who comes into our lives, but we do have control over who we allow to walk away from us." Please, get to know the men and women of God who come into your life and preserve that relationship.

Story - The Golden Rule

One day, a mother happened to overhear a group of little girls excitedly concocting a scheme of revenge against another little girl, who apparently had done something very mean. She was grieved to find her own child among the chief conspirators.

"Why, my dear!" she said, taking her child aside, "It seems to me you are going to do to Lottie just what you don't want her to do to you. I don't think this is the Golden Rule-is it?"

"Well, mama," said the child, "the Golden Rule is all right for Sunday, but for every day I'd rather have an eye for an eye and a tooth for a tooth."

I wander how many of you operate from this premise. Does your faith and salvation work outside of the sanctuary or only when you are in the presence of other believers?

Background on the book of Kings

The book of Kings is historical in nature and gives insights into the activities of the Children of Israel as a united and divided kingdom. King David serves as the model king simply because he displayed the true meaning of faith, worship, and praise. The covenant community was confronted with a series of adversaries, and they were triumphant on all fronts as long as they adhered to the prophetic. In addition, Israel often faced various forms of challenges, and they succumbed to idolatry and corruption in far too many instances. Therefore, God seemed to utilize a proven method of getting their attention via a famine. The primary theme of the book predicates itself upon the sovereignty of God.

Problem

It appears to me a large number of people are laying claim to being a believer or follower of Christ but fail to display a noteworthy character similar to Christ. This occurs from magnifying the challenges of life much more than the faith that is extended to us as a spiritual tool for overcoming. This is because Satan has masterfully caused a spiritual disconnection, whereby you fail to see God delights in bringing forth deliverance in diverse forms on behalf of the righteous.

Contemporary realities

- ➤ The text opens by mentioning the town of Gilgal, which was located south of Shiloh in the Tribe of Ephraim.
- ➤ The text points out there were unusual circumstances occurring as a result of a famine. The Hebrew term *ra'ab* refers to hunger, lack of food, lack of God's word, or simply being depraved of necessities spread over a specific area and a specific amount of time.
- ➤ Famine in the land is an indication that it was widespread. It should also be noted famines are spiritual and physical realities, but someone must be called to address the plight at the end of the day.
- ➤ Meanwhile, the *Sons of the Prophets* denote a pool of men in fellowship who were divinely called and undergoing training under the tutelage of Elisha and other seasoned men of faith. Good and effective leadership has a mandate to produce new leadership. Bad times affect both the righteous and unrighteous, but God is spiritually mandated to address the plight of the righteous because they are on assignment.
- ➤ Elisha felt compassion for their plight (hunger) while recognizing their faithfulness. Therefore, he instructed his servant, Gehazi to "Set on the large pot, and boil stew for the sons of the prophets." This phrase is used metaphorically and literally because literally sitting on a hot pot can cause physical harm. However, this phrase may also suggest divine favor upon this undertaking.
- ➤ A boiling pot needs ingredients in order to feed the hungry. Meanwhile, one of the prophets

went to get herbs for seasoning, and apparently, he did not pay close attention or did not know what he gathered. You know there are nutritional and poisonous herbs such as mushrooms.

➢ Sometimes, a good deed/gesture can result in deadly consequences.

➢ The wild gourd was cut and placed in the stew. This leaves our imagination to wonder what else was contained in the pot such as lentil, lamb, goat, and other vegetables.

➢ One of them detected the presence of death once they commenced to serve the stew and eat. Therefore, they had the presence of mind (prophets in training) to summon the Man of God by saying "O man of God, there is death in the pot." Can you detect death before it overtakes you or those around you?

➢ Elisha was anointed and on assignment to serve on behalf of the King of Glory, and seemed undisturbed by their finding because he is the one who was inspired to initiate the feeding. Something external has to be entered into the equation in order for death to be rebuked. In this instance, he simply used a little flour to add to the dish. This gesture and faith caused him to say, "Pour some out for the men that they may eat."

➢ Now, what would you do in this situation? Will you refrain from eating or stand on the word of faith? There is life and instruction in the Word of God spoken by the Man/Woman of God. Remember there must be some participation in order for your faith to reward you.

➢ This story concludes by reaffirming what Elisha already knew. What appeared to be deadly resulted in causing no harm, what so ever?

➢ Unfortunately, we live in an era, wherein those with oversight of our foods, such as the Food and

Drug Administration and U.S. Agricultural Department know that plenty of our food is filled with chemicals that cause death without calling attention to this reality?

Now, let me shift to the next story, verses 42-44 wherein we will observe a lack of food amongst the prophets. However, the willing contribution of a single man was sufficient for the man of faith (Elisha) to utilize and cause something greater to unfold. You will observe the sequence of events is listed below:

Facts and realities surrounding the story

> Both Elijah and Elisha are archetypes of Christ because they were mobile and interacted with people in order to demonstrate our God is engaged in His Creation, integrally.
> This story opens by identifying another town within the tribe of Ephraim, Baal-shalishah. The name of this town reflects the culture and religion (Baalism) wherein Israel was located, but it mandated to worship and serve the true and living God.
> The area was experiencing a prolonged famine, but interestingly, God provided food on behalf of the righteous. An unidentified man came bearing food, namely twenty (redemption) loaves of barley and grain to Elisha and the community as part of his obedience to the law regarding the First fruits.
> Time and time again, I have seen the best come out of people during crises.
> The term *First fruits* are spiritual in nature even though we see it manifested in physical ways that benefit others. Biblically, this term instructs the faith community to offer or sacrifice the earliest crops/harvest unto the Lord by giving them to the priest or prophet. In addition, you will display obedience and obtain

82

Favor from God for your household and the community. The first of everything belongs to the Lord.

➢ This gesture had other ramifications because Elisha had the oversight of providing food and assistance to others under his watch. We notice Elisha receiving the food and immediately disbursing it to those affected by the famine. This reminds me of how my father would often go places and be given food or placed in a position of honor. He would always consider others i.e. children or other less prominent individuals before eating instead of immediately partaking or sitting in the place of honor.

➢ Elisha disbursed the food because he already knew the source of the food stemmed from the Most High God and not the person who brought it.

➢ Gehazi gives a typical response in light of the number of hungry people sitting before them. What good is this little food in the midst of all these hungry men? Remember there is always something you can do, refrain from embrace doubt or skepticism.

➢ Elisha was a man of faith and destiny therefore; he focused on bringing hope in despair and joy in sadness. He repeated his instruction by saying, "Give them to the men, that they may eat, for thus says the Lord." Can you declare the oracles and blessings of the Lord even though circumstances may not look favorable at the moment?

➢ Elisha went on to say not only will they eat, but there will be food left over. God's provision and intervention is designed to always have more than enough upon declaring His word, but you cannot experience this grace unless you act in obedience and faith.

➤ They followed the instruction of the man of God and, surely enough, there was food left over. This demonstration of deliverance served as a model/example of a miracle Jesus performed many years later in Galilee.

Contemporary realities

➤ In the text, we saw a couple of illustrations that could have easily resulted in death, but the Word of God was spoken and rebuked what appeared to be inevitable. Today, there are millions of people living in the presence of death due to greed and mismanagement in both the public and private sectors.

➤ The western world consumes most of the supplies and products on the market but fails to genuinely show compassion to the disinherited or least of these amongst us.

➤ The media and many of our conversations tend to promote or accentuate negative situations and a pessimistic view instead of allowing God to use you to bring hope and optimism. Why do we think and act the way we do?

➤ The form of evil, distress, trouble, and adversity may vary, but there will be favorable results when the Word of God is spoken and acted upon.

➤ Death is in the food we eat, like the pot of stew in our story, and this is due to commercialization and chemicals in the products all under the banner of preservation. Death is in the water we drink, such as we see recently observed in Flint, MI. Things are done out of convenience and habits versus what is ethical, wholesome, and prudent.

➤ Why would there be a person in your community or family living in poverty when you have resources to share? What if every millionaire and billionaire personally adopted 100 people and monitored their lives until their conditions changed. Instead, we waste time in foolishness by compiling the billionaires' list.

➢ What if 1000 people with meager means shared a minimum of $10.00 per week with our ministry and allowed those funds go toward helping someone who is hungry, thirsty, naked, stranger, sick, or imprisoned? This gesture is helpful and would go a long way.

➢ Large problems do not go away by simply wishing or looking for someone else to do it, but rather everyone must participate in some fashion if we want to see deliverance.

➢ Selfish and callous people cannot be blessed. Elisha paid attention to Elijah giving and caring, and that is what he picked up and implemented.

➢ Shakespeare once said, "Tis not enough to help the feeble up, But to support him after."

➢ I am both disappointed and inspired based upon what I see around me. I see lazy people in my community giving into their situations as if they have to take whatever is dished to them, but I am also inspired because I see President Barack Obama, an African American emerging as the 44th President of the most powerful nation on earth.

➢ He was elected President for a second term; however, these realities yet stare us in the face. For example, we are part of the most racist nation on earth, constitute the largest number of incarcerated prisoners. Furthermore, African Americans head that list. We are the recipients of the worst lending practices to poor people. Moreover, teen pregnancy, poor health, violence and religious concepts enslave us, etc.

➢ Barack Obama's escalation to this esteemed office partially reminds me of the bumblebee as a result of contradicting aerodynamics and flies

85

with *tee nainchy* wings and a big, fat body. Do you understand what I am saying? He is not supposed to be president on the basis of the convention and psyche of the majority in this nation, but look at what God has allowed before our very eyes,

➢ Dead food, lead-infested houses, dilapidated communities, abusive relationships, low self-esteem, poisoned foods, inoperable organs, deadly weapons at our disposal, drug and alcohol abuse, car accidents, burned-down houses, and being exposed to the elements that are designed to kill you.

➢ This sermon can definitely relate to the current water crisis in Flint, Michigan where lead in the water supply is causing sickness and potential death. The Governor and other officials knew what was going on politically and opted to turn the other way until it was widely exposed. Therefore, like the man of God, we refuse to ignore this reality and chose to coordinate a truckload of water be delivered to Flint, MI.

➢ Amazingly, God allows evil and shameful acts such as these to occur. However, more importantly, we have the resources and wherewithal to correct this problem. Therefore, we cannot ignore what is happening.

➢ Many of you have overcome these and other adversities, not because of luck and chance, but it was because of God's amazing grace utilizing others like you and I to help make a difference. Faith and works must come together.

➢ Dr. Howard Thurman eloquently said, "When the condition for growth is met, then growth will occur."

➢ The global community has evolved into a disheartening sight where the quest for power and territorial expansion at the expense of others is causing a disproportionate number of deaths and destruction.

➢ The Word of God is tailor made to address and transform conditions that appear too lifeless in the grasp of death because life is greater than death and freedom is more powerful than bondage.

➢ If you live and breathe negative thoughts and succumb to disheartening realities, then you are on the course of death, not life. Most of you get the appropriate return based upon what you have invested.

Proposition

How many of you ever found yourself trying to impress someone, and you were not noticed or simply ignored after all you did? Being ignored is a miserable feeling, and no one welcomes that reality. I firmly believe when the conditions for deliverance are met, then God will send His messenger to that situation. Therefore, I want to suggest four unique perspectives surrounding your situations and your opportunities through opening the ears and hearts to the liberating Word of God. This will allow a foundation of righteousness be established in realizing what is meant by demonstrations of faith and deliverance.

Body

1. The first perspective hinges upon realizing that everything happens under the watchful eyes of God, and there is no need to panic when adversities strike. It is best to gather in the circles of life (School of Prophets) and **hear** what the Lord has to say in that instance, so that you will be positioned to receive what is

necessary and rewarding for you and others in the school of deliverance.

2. The second perspective revolves around your ability to realize your current realities should not overshadow your spiritual destiny in terms of allowing yourself to spiritually **see** where you are as nothing more than a conditioning of where God wants to take you. Everything happens for the good of those who are grounded in His righteousness.

3. The third perspective centers on being awakened to the fact that everyone must be involved if they really want to see positive results. This comes by means of becoming a faithful **participant** in the avenues God has permitted to assist you, which will establish you in the faith and heighten your testimony in the Kingdom of God.

4. The fourth and final perspective has to do with displaying the appropriate spirit before and after your challenges causing you to enthusiastically **celebrate/praise** God for the wonderful things He has done on behalf of you and others. Consequently, this will allow you to gain the favor of God and position you for continual blessings.

Conclusion & Story

I have presented four sermons with circumstances that interrupted the normal course of events. I have also tried to demonstrate God has a unique way of sending the additional assistance needed to take you through and beyond your challenges when you faithfully listen and participate. Elisha was a model servant of God and never allowed difficult matters to dictate the outcome because he had a great teacher and an attentive ear to the Spirit.

Do not waste time glorifying your adversities because they will keep coming. Instead, I admonish you to come to appreciate the truth in knowing the Word of God brings light and life

.

Let me close with this story. A father with a quarrelsome family thought he might more readily prevail by an example after having tried in vain to reconcile them through words. Therefore, he called his sons and bade them to lay a bundle of sticks before him. Then, having tied them up into a fagot, he told each lad after the other to take it up and break it. They all tried but tried in vain. Then, he untied the fagot and gave them the sticks to break one by one. They did this with the greatest ease. Then, the father said, "Thus, my sons, as long as you remain united, you are a match for all your enemies; but you are undone if you differ and separate."

Leaders will come and go like we saw in the case of Elijah and Elisha. Trouble will come and go like we saw in these stories. However, the Word of God is faithful, eternal, and has the ability to transform every situation. I probably will not be here as long as I have already been here, but the Word of God is comforting and eternal throughout all generations. I want to attract followers and leaders in the Kingdom of God; whereby, all of you will come to appreciate **Demonstrations of Faith and Deliverance.** God bless you!

www.ingramcontent.com/pod-product-compliance
Lightning Source LLC
LaVergne TN
LVHW051814080426
835513LV00017B/1945